Coyright © 2024

All rights reserved. No part of this publication may be reproduced, distributed, or transmitted in any form or by any means, including photocopying, recording, or other electronic or mechanical methods, without the prior written permission of the publisher, except in the case of brief quotations embodied in critical reviews and certain other noncommercial uses permitted by copyright law.

Join Sami, a spirited boy with big dreams, as he discovers the magic of Black History Month, embraces his heritage, and dances his way to victory with the help of his playful puppy, Max, in a heartwarming celebration of culture, courage, and creativity!

THE CLASSROOM DISCOVERY

Sami sat in the classroom, his yellow shirt bright against his desk, as his teacher explained the importance of Black History Month. She told stories of leaders like Martin Luther King Jr., who fought for equality, while Sami listened with wide eyes and a growing sense of pride.

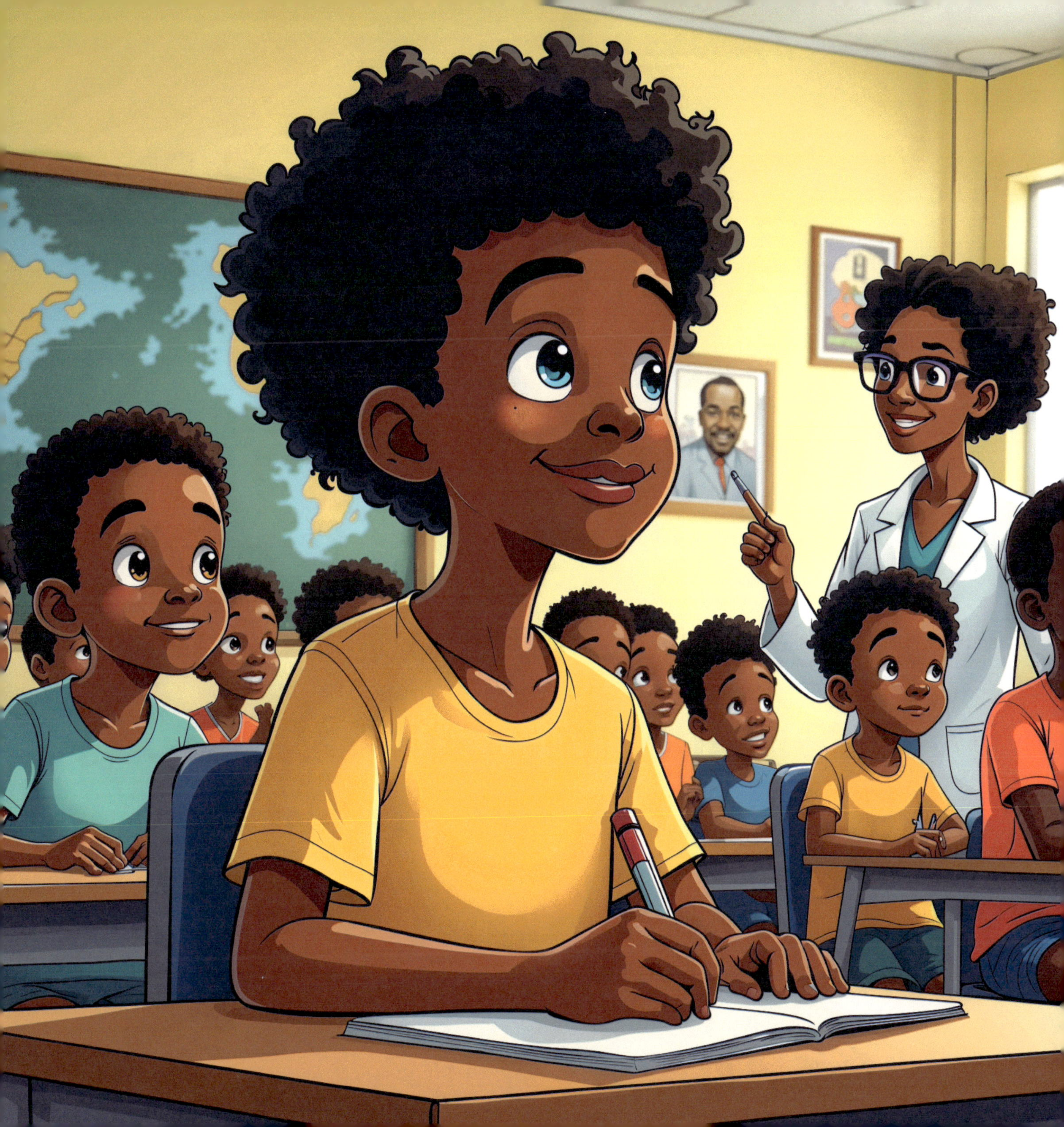

The teacher explained that Black History Month celebrates achievements and culture, with festivals, music, and dance. She encouraged the class to explore their heritage and participate in events. Sami felt inspired, imagining ways to celebrate his own history.

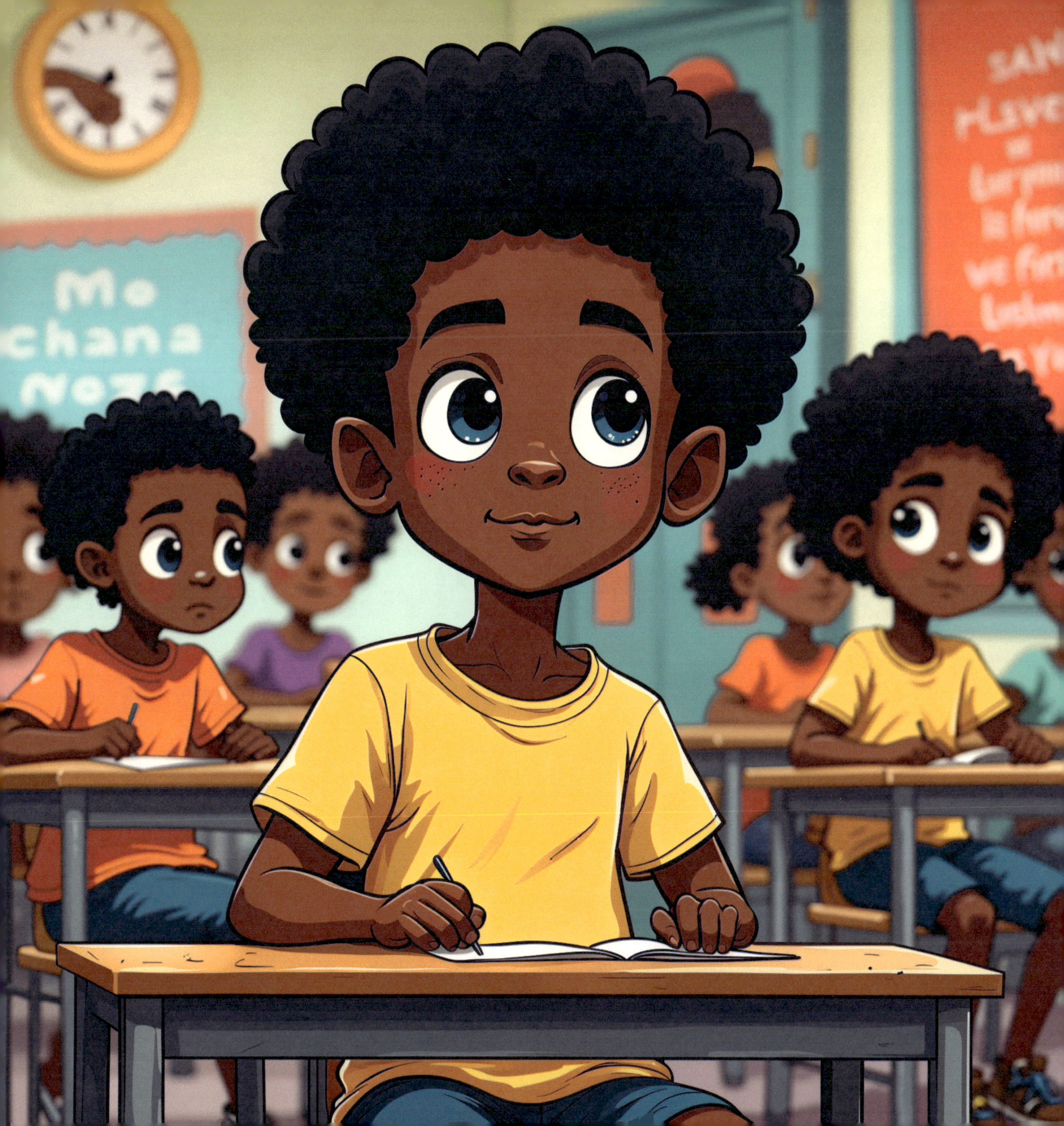
Mo
chana

When class ended, Sami left with excitement bubbling in his chest. As he walked home, he spotted a poster announcing a Black History Month festival featuring a dance competition. His heart raced-he wanted to enter and show his pride through dance.

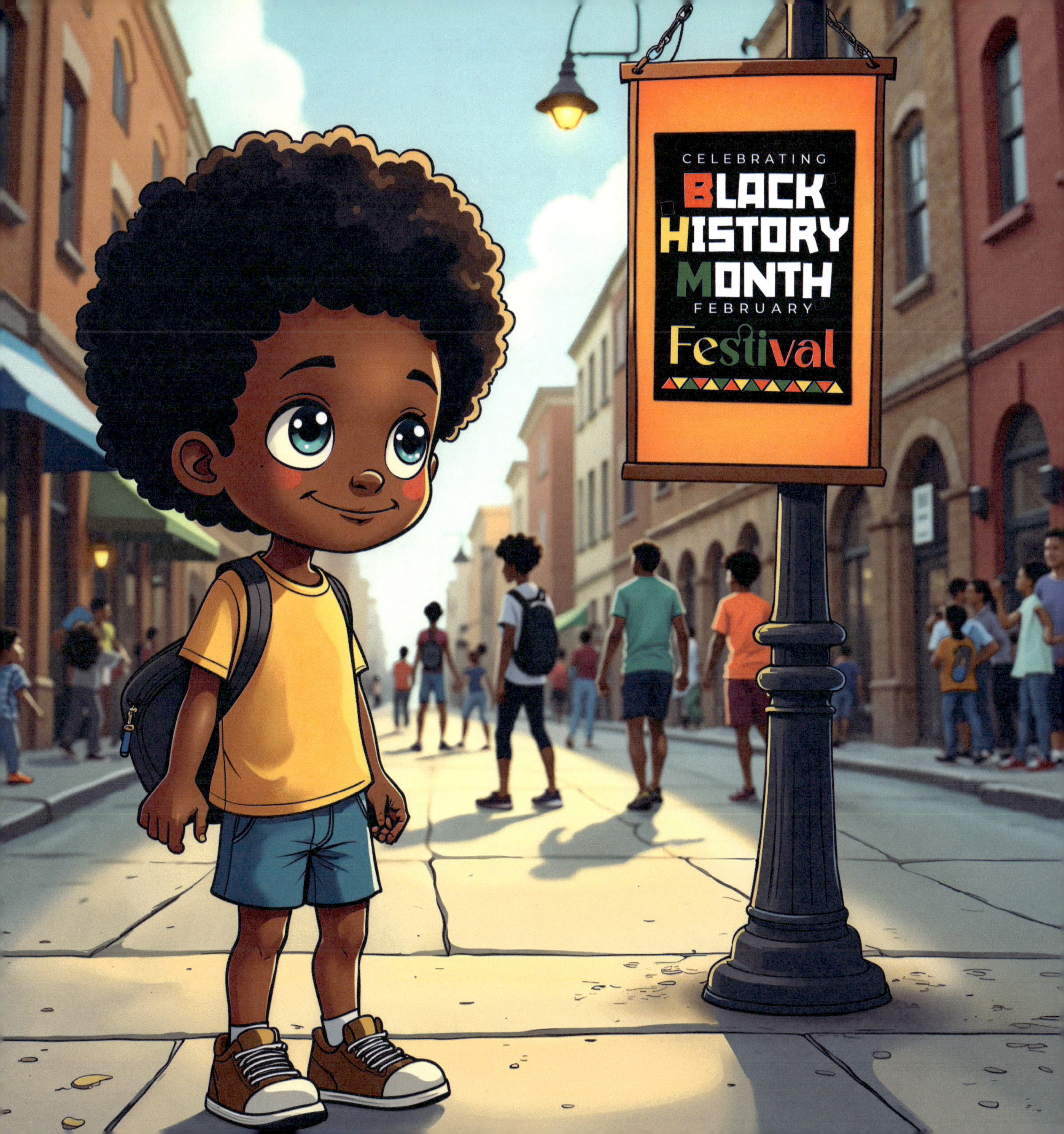
CELEBRATING
BLACK
HISTORY
MONTH
FEBRUARY
Festival

THE PERFECT OUTFIT

At home, Sami searched for the perfect outfit for the competition. His closet was full, but nothing seemed right. Frustrated, he slumped on his bed. His mother entered, her smile soft. 'Check the old trunk in the basement,' she suggested. 'Your grandfather's suit might inspire you.'

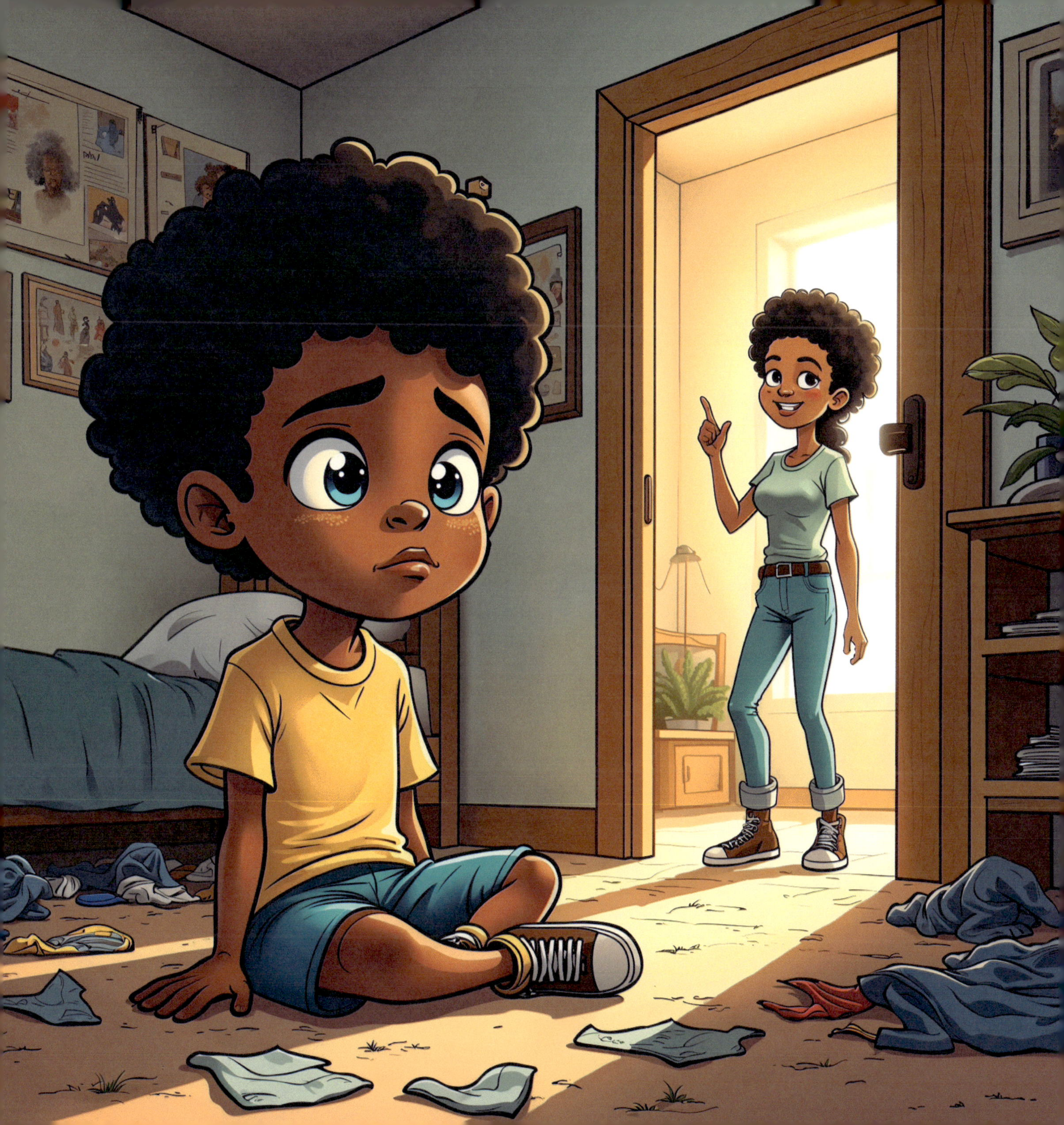

Sami hurried to the basement, where he opened the old trunk. Inside lay a formal black suit, tailored with elegant lines and fine stitching. His eyes widened in awe. As he tried it on, he felt an unexplainable confidence and connection to his heritage.

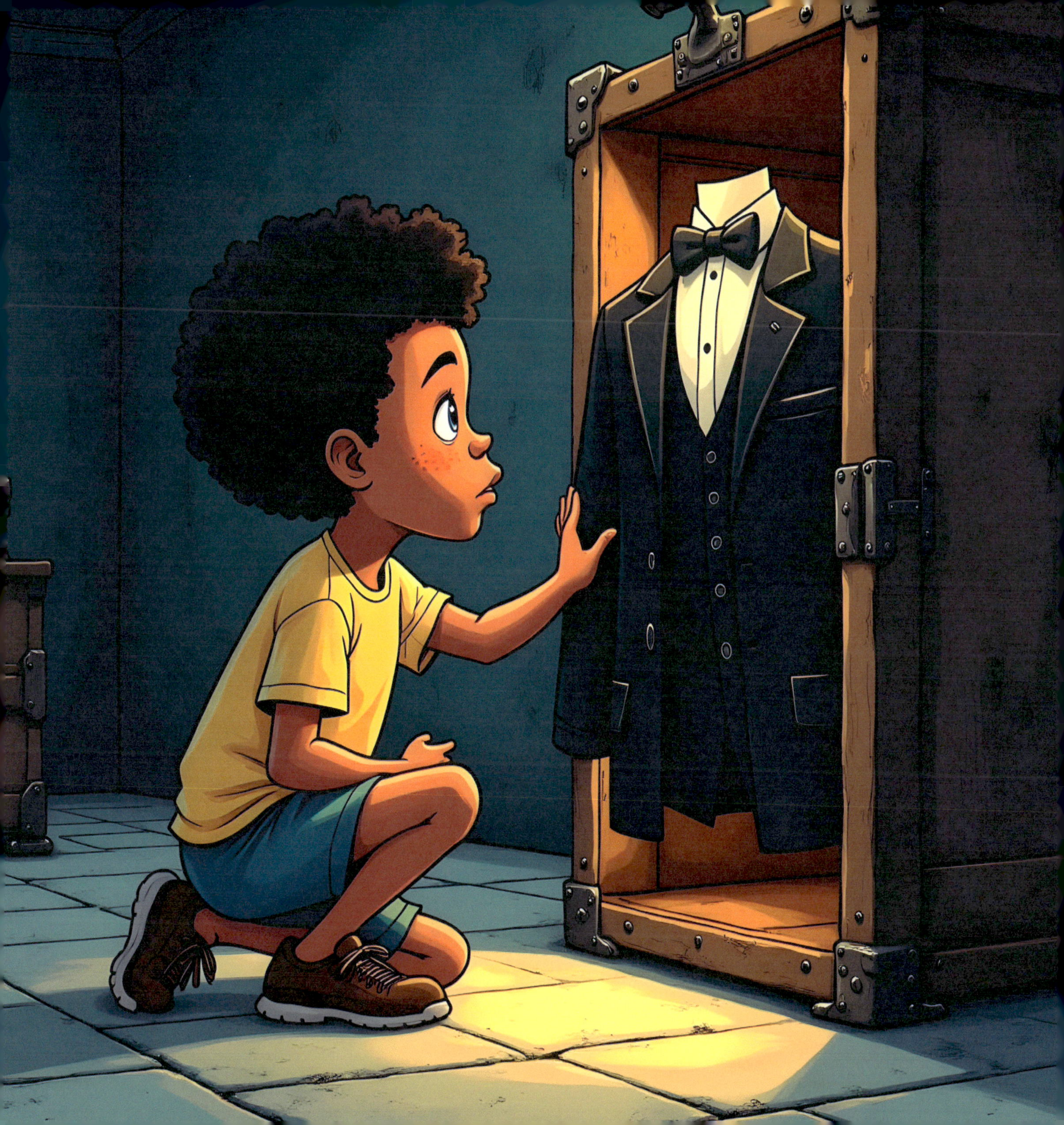

Though he had the perfect outfit, Sami still wondered what kind of dance to perform. His white puppy, Max, bounded in, wagging his tail. Watching Max's playful energy, Sami grinned. 'I'll dance like you!' he declared, petting Max with newfound determination.

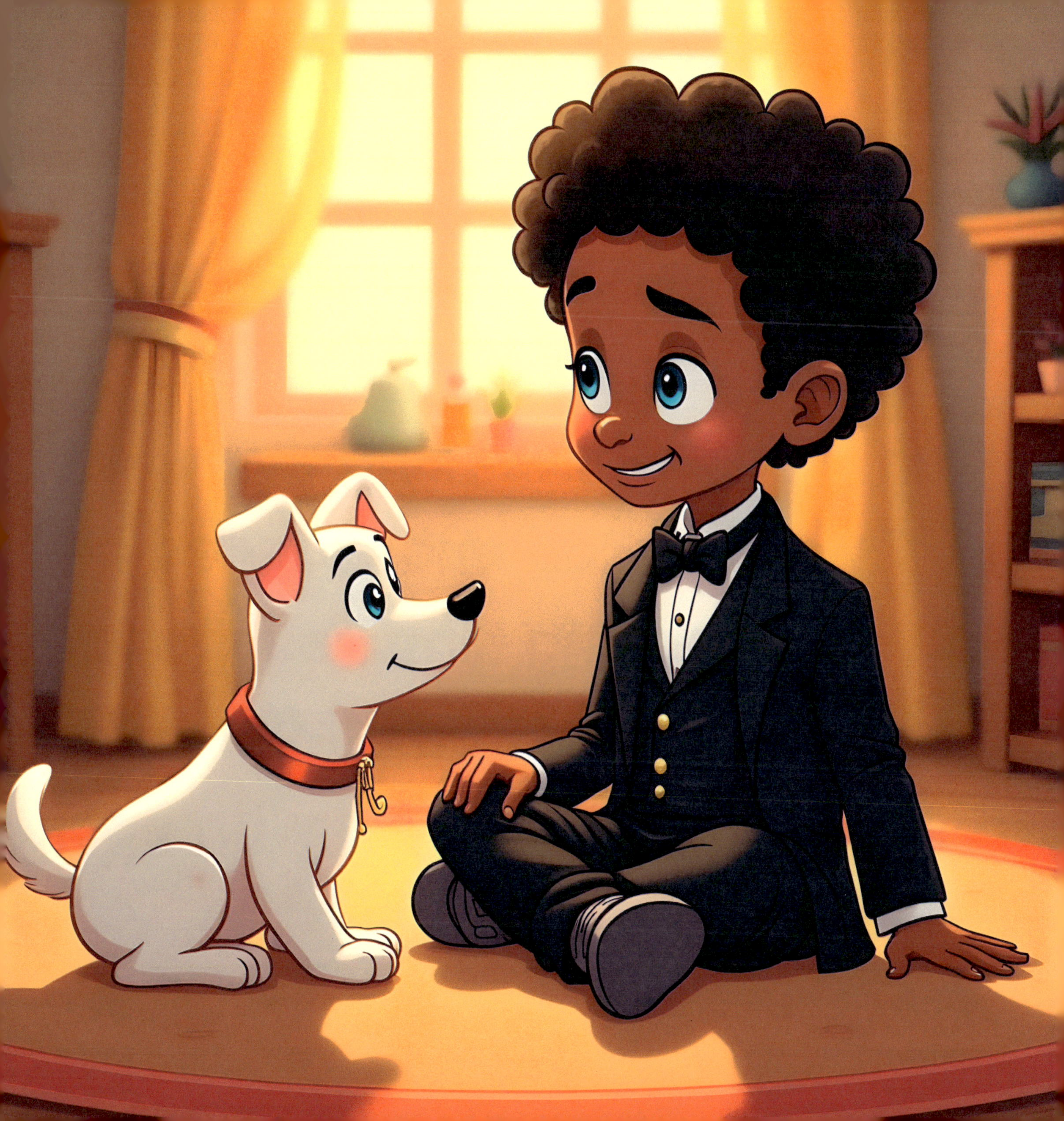

PRACTICE MAKES PERFECT

In the garden, Sami practiced his dance inspired by Max. He stumbled, tripped, and even fell, but Max barked and wagged his tail, encouraging him. Despite the setbacks, Sami kept trying, his determination growing with each step.

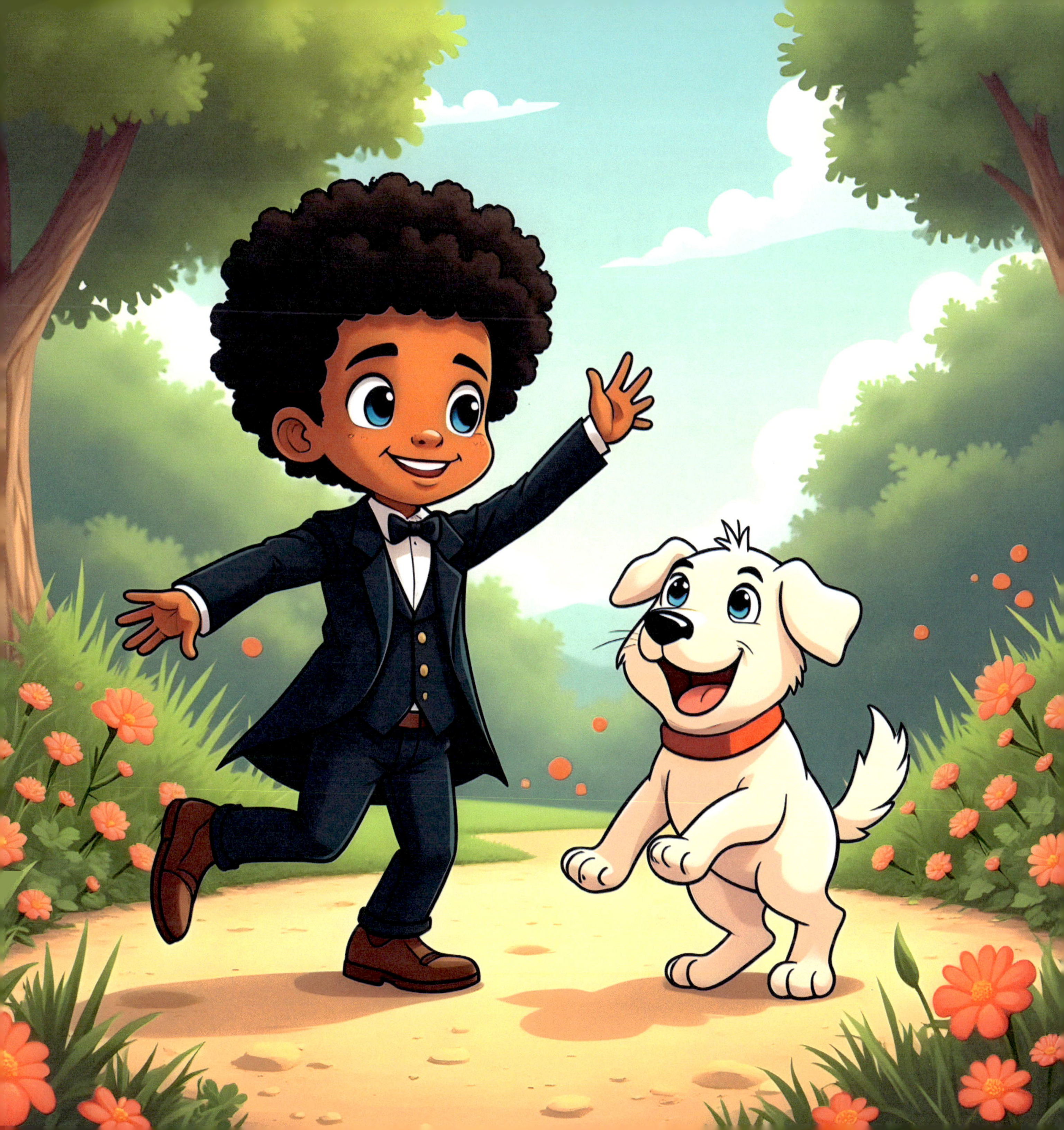

As the sun set, Sami finally perfected his routine. The moonlit garden saw his graceful steps and playful hops come together in harmony. Max barked in approval as Sami spun with confidence, a wide smile on his face.

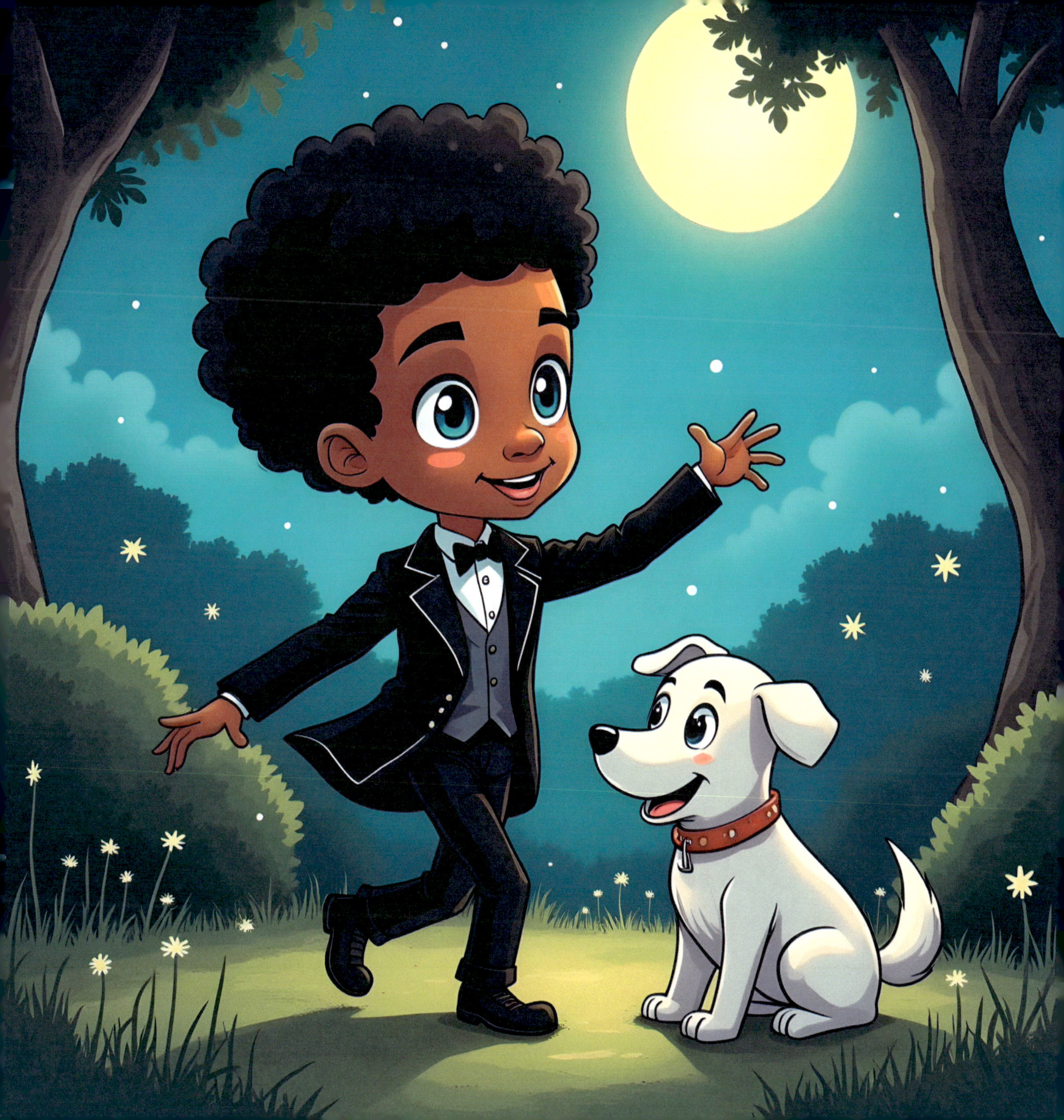

That night, Sami went to bed exhausted but happy. His routine was ready, and he felt connected to both his puppy and his heritage. 'Tomorrow's going to be amazing,' he whispered, drifting into dreams filled with dances and cheers.

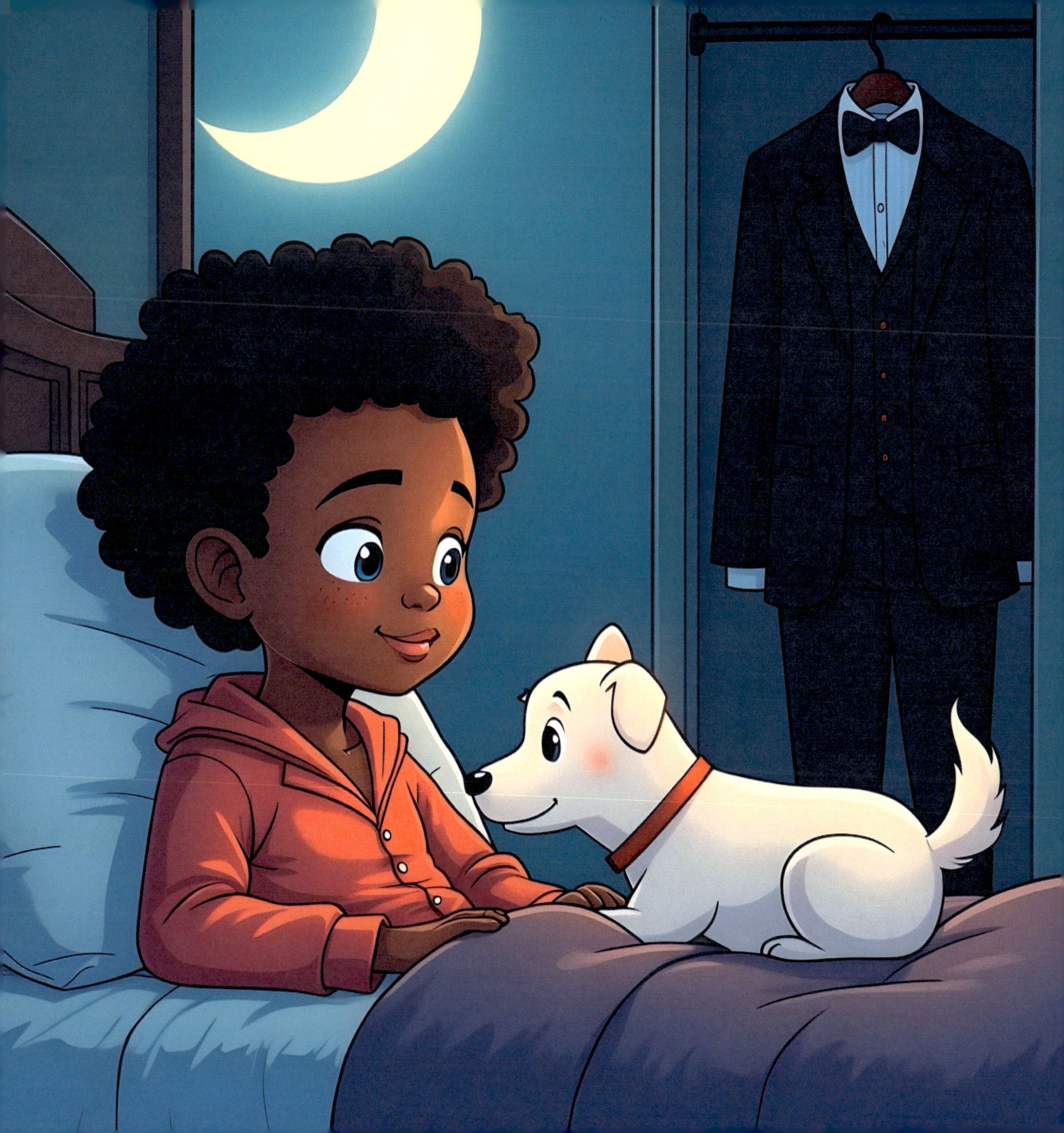

THE BIG DAY

At the festival, vibrant colors, lively music, and cheers filled the air. Sami's heart pounded as he stood backstage, wearing his grandfather's elegant black suit. When his turn came, he stepped onto the stage, ready to shine.

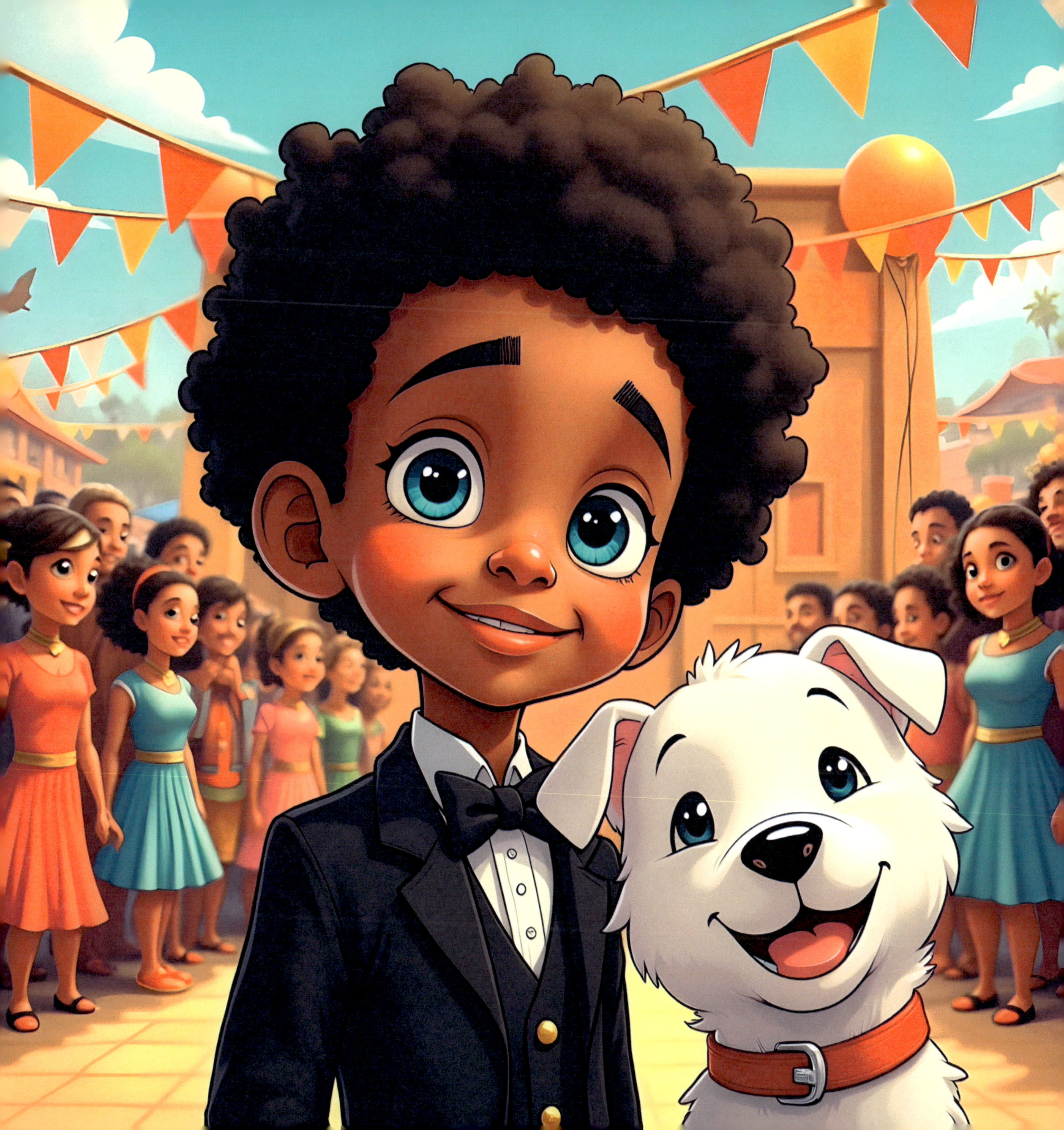

Sami danced with energy and passion, mixing playful moves inspired by Max with elegant steps. The crowd clapped and cheered, captivated by his unique routine. Sami's smile grew with every spin and hop, his confidence shining.

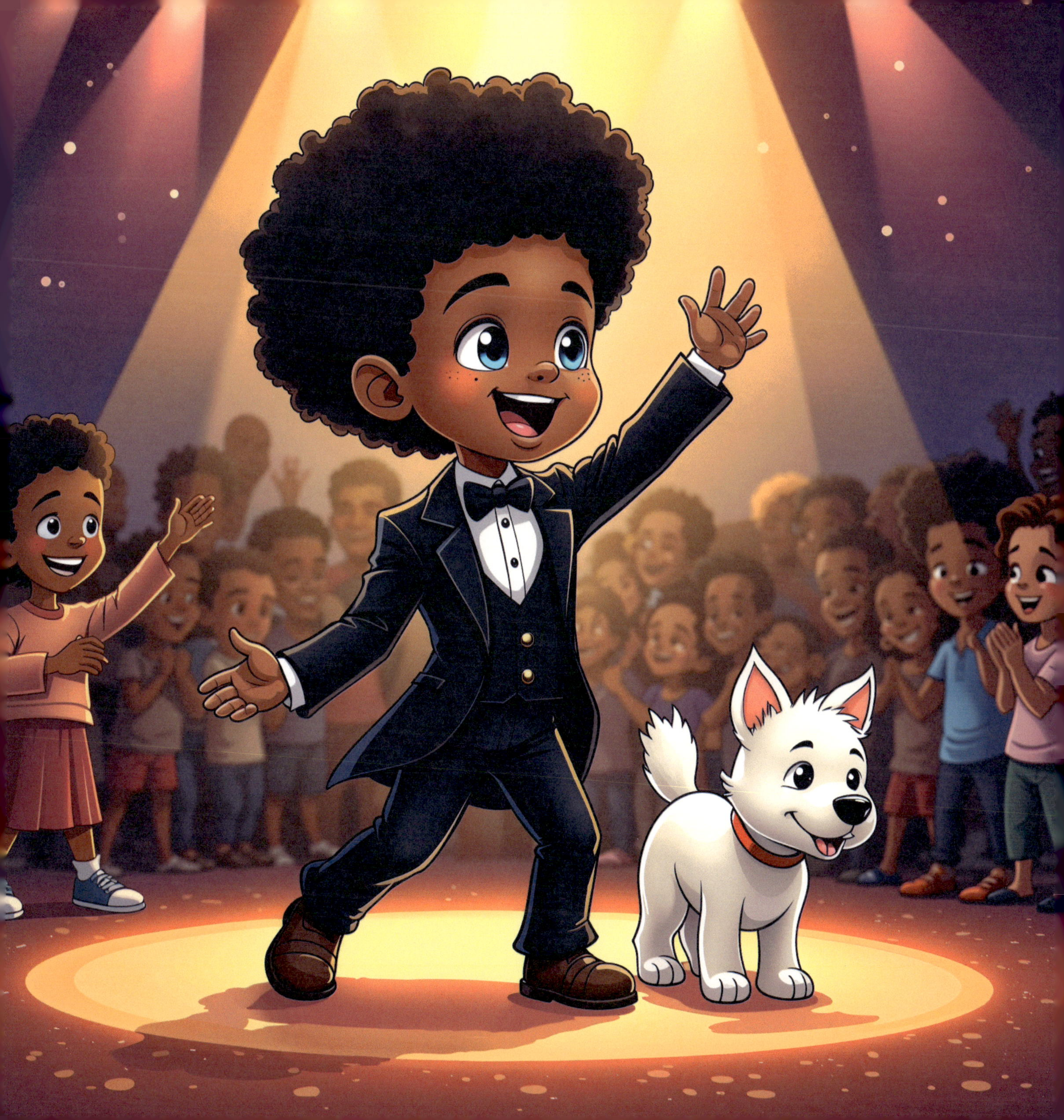

When the competition ended, Sami was declared the winner of the 'Best Dance' trophy. He stood on stage, holding the trophy high, pride glowing in his eyes. The applause reminded him that believing in himself had made all the difference.

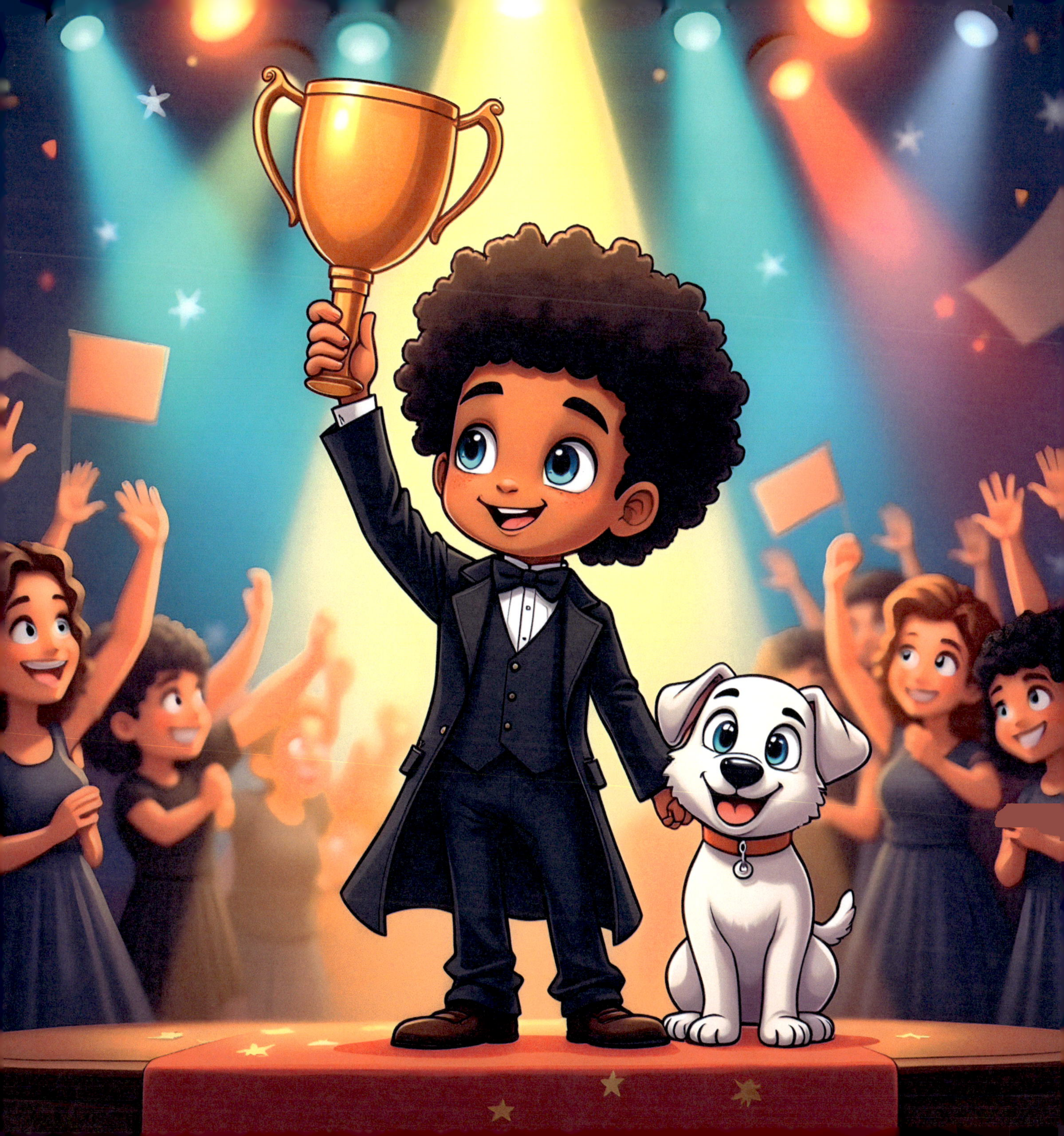

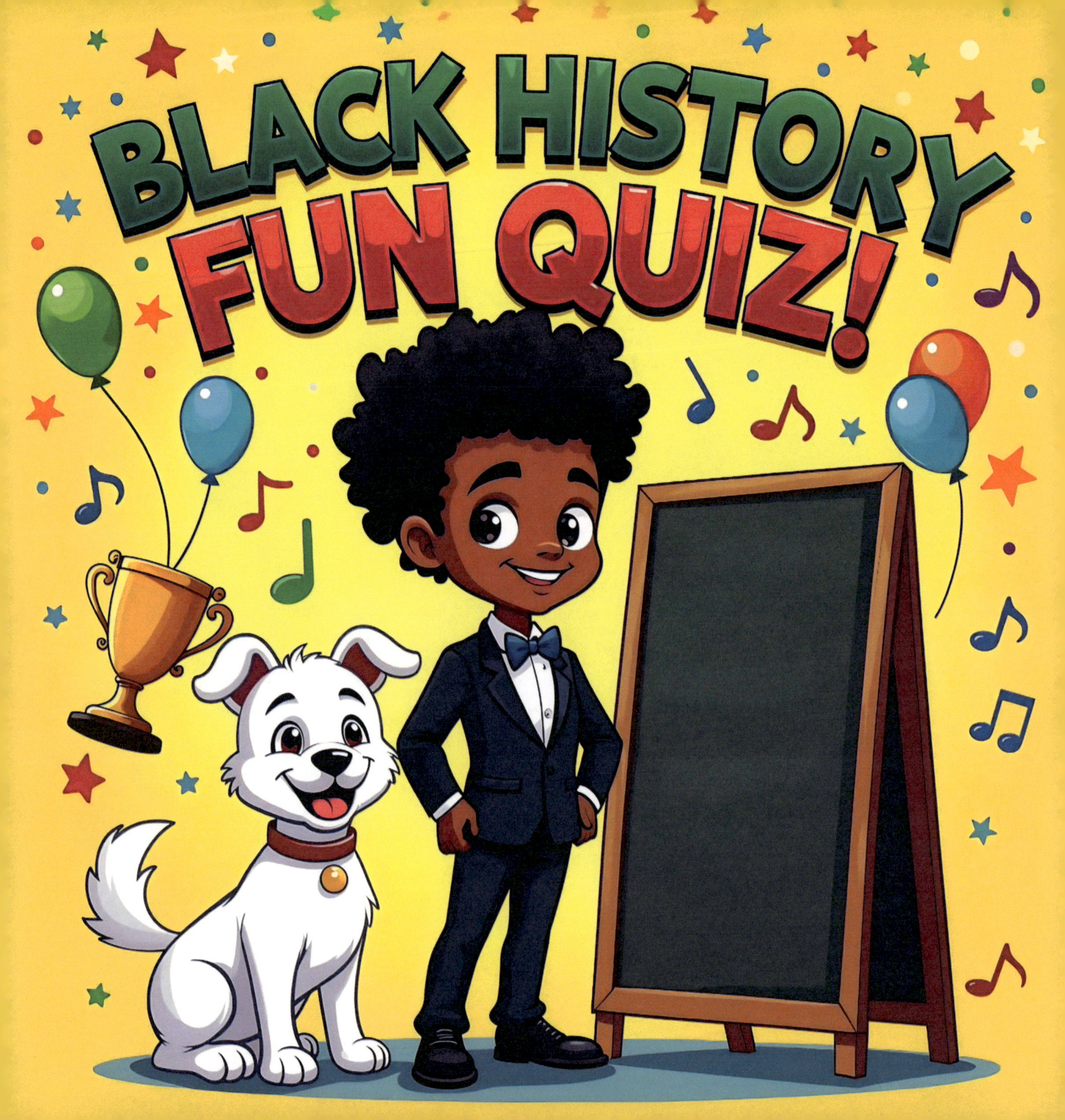

BLACK HISTORY FUN QUIZ!

What did Sami's teacher talk about?

A) Black History Month

B) Dance Classes

C) Science Projects

What was the competition about?

A) Best Dance

B) Best Costume

C) Best Drawing

What outfit did Sami wear?

A) Black Suit

B) Yellow Shirt

C) Blue Jacket

What did Sami win?

A) A Trophy

B) A Medal

C) A Ribbon

Made in the USA
Columbia, SC
05 February 2025